DREAMS

HIRO

To my dearest kitty,

"Let our dreams come true..."

Contents

PREFACE

At night we all go to sleep and sometimes we see some imaginary things about us or someone we know or don't which we call "Dreams". But there is a thing I want to point out, we don't occasionally dream, we dream every day. But we don't remember it. We usually dream about falling, scary dreams, flying...etc. Are these dreams trying to tell us something, do these dreams have meanings, if yes what do these dreams mean? Let's find out.

Acknowledgements

Thank you for helping me all my closest ones...

I

Introduction

A dream is an experience of imagined images, voices, or other sensations during sleep. Dreams often portray events that are impossible or unlikely in reality and are usually outside the control of the dreamer. Many people report experiencing strong emotions while dreaming and frightening or upsetting dreams are referred to as nightmares. the scientific disciple of dream research is oneirology.

Dreams have a long history both as a subject of conjecture and a source of inspiration (artistic or otherwise). Throughout history, people have sought meaning in dreams. They have been described physiologically as a response to neural processes during sleep, psychologically as reflections of the unconscious, and spiritually as messages from god or predictions of the future (oneiromancy).

Most scientists believe that almost all humans dream with approximately the same frequency. Even those who rarely recall dreams report having them if awakened during rapi8d eye movement (REM) sleep. Dreaming in animals varies from species to species.

II

What are Dreams?

At its most basic level, a dream is a collection of images, impressions, events, and emotions that we experience during sleep. Sometimes dreams have real storylines, with plots and characters that could be plucked from a movie screen. Other times dreams are more impressionistic, filled with emotions and visual imagery.

Typically, a person will spend two hours or more a night dreaming, experiencing somewhere between 3-6 dreams over the course of a night's rest. Most dreams appear to last from 5-20 minutes.

I often hear people say, "I don't dream." You may not remember your dreams, but that doesn't mean you're not having them. Dreaming is a universal human experience. The truth is, the vast majority of dreams we experience will—for most of us—never be remembered. Memories of dreams usually fade very quickly after we awaken.

III

Why do we Dream?

The why of dreaming is one of the great mysteries of sleep. There are many different theories about why dreaming happens. There are some scientists who think that dreaming has no specific underlying purpose, that our dreams might be a by-product of other things going on in the brain during sleep. But many scientists studying sleep and dreams believe there is a primary purpose to our dreams. Different theories suggest that dreams are:

- A way to process memory and learning, moving memories from short-term to long-term storage and giving the brain a clean slate before the next waking day
- A way to maintain emotional balance, by working through difficult, complicated, unsettling thoughts, emotions, and experiences
- A different state of consciousness that unites past, present, and future—to process information from the first two, and prepare for the third
- A kind of dress rehearsal for the brain, to prepare itself to face threats, dangers, and challenges in waking life
- The brain responding to biochemical changes and

electrical impulses that occur during sleep

There may not be a single answer to why we dream. Our dreams might serve several purposes at once.

IV

Why can't we remember our Dreams?

The ability to recall dreams varies a lot from one individual to another. Some people can regularly remember their dreams, while others may have only hazy recollections of themes or subjects in their dreams—or no recollection at all. There are a number of possible explanations for this. Studies suggest dream recall may be linked to patterns of activity in the brain. Our ability to recall our dreams may be influenced by interpersonal attachment styles—the way we tend to form bonds with other people in our lives. Changing hormone levels throughout the night might also have a role in our ability to recall our dreams. During REM sleep—a time of active dreaming—levels of the hormone cortisol are high, and may interfere with communication between areas of the brain that are involved in memory consolidation.

Our most active dreaming occurs during REM sleep. Adults spend roughly 25 percent of their sleep time in REM sleep, with longer periods of REM sleep occurring later in the night and in the early morning.

REM sleep is one part of the normal sleep cycle. In addition to REM sleep, sleep cycles contain three other stages of sleep. Dreaming can occur in every stage of sleep. Dreams during REM sleep appear to be more visually vivid, bizarre, and narratively-driven than dreams during other sleep stages.

Have you ever woken and not been able to move or speak? This scary sleep phenomenon is indirectly related to dreaming. During REM sleep, the body goes into a state of temporary paralysis, a condition known as REM atonia. This appears to be the body's way of protecting itself during dreaming. REM atonia keeps us from acting out physically in response to dreams. Think of some of the scary or exciting dreams you've experienced. Maybe you've been flying over a mountain range, or been chased by a masked intruder. Imagine if you could respond physically to these dream experiences. You might fly yourself right out of bed onto the floor.

It's possible to awaken and still be in a state of sleep paralysis. This can be a really scary experience, particularly the first time it happens. Waking in sleep paralysis is a sign that your body may not be making smooth transitions between the stages of sleep. This can be the result of stress, sleep deprivation, other sleep disorders including narcolepsy, as well as a side effect of medications or over-consumption of drugs or alcohol.

V

Phases of Sleep

There are five phases of sleep in a sleep cycle:

Stage 1: Light sleep, slow eye movement, and reduced muscle activity. This stage forms 4 to 5 percent of total sleep.

Stage 2: Eye movement stops and brain waves become slower, with occasional bursts of rapid waves called sleep spindles. This stage forms 45 to 55 percent of total sleep.

Stage 3: Extremely slow brain waves called delta waves begin to appear, interspersed with smaller, faster waves. This accounts for 4 to 6 percent of total sleep.

Stage 4: The brain produces delta waves almost exclusively. It is difficult to wake someone during stages 3 and 4, which together are called "deep sleep." There is no eye movement or muscle activity. People awakened while in deep sleep do not adjust immediately and often feel disoriented for several minutes after waking up. This forms 12 to 15 percent of total sleep.

Stage 5: This stage is known as rapid eye movement (REM). Breathing becomes more rapid, irregular, and shallow, eyes jerk rapidly in various directions, and limb muscles become temporarily paralyzed. Heart rate increases, blood pressure rises, and males develop penile erections. When people awaken during REM sleep, they often describe bizarre and illogical tales. These are dreams. This stage accounts for 20 to 25 percent of total sleep time.

VI

Types of Dreams

There are a variety of different dreams we are capable of experiencing:

1. Daydreams: Daydreaming refers to a series of thoughts that distract you from the outside world, making you less aware of your surroundings. Daydreams occur while we are awake and are produced by the brain's default mode network in the brain in response to a lack of stimulation. Types of daydreaming include dysphoric, escapism, fantasy, rumination, and visualization.

2. False-awakening dreams: These dreams are when the sleeper believes they have woken up from a sleep session but are still in the middle of a dream. False-awakening dreams are a hybrid state that overlaps with wakefulness and sleep, commonly linked to sleep paralysis or lucid dreams.

3. Healing dreams: Healing dreams are dreams where the dreamer can heal others, or has a supernatural power like telekinesis or telepathy. Healing dreams can bring feelings of balance and reconciliation. They can help you facilitate a sense of peace or purpose through your

unconscious mind.

4. Lucid dreams: Lucid dreaming is a dream where the sleeper becomes aware that they are dreaming and can retain some control of their body and thoughts within the dream.

5. Nightmares: Nightmares are fear-inducing dreams. This dream state is the brain's way of processing life's daily stressors. Some common causes of nightmares are poor eating habits, previous traumatic events, illness, sleep deprivation, sleep disorders, or medication.

6. Prophetic dreams: In prophetic dreams, people see future events occur before they happen in real life. Some believe these dreams mean a person has predicted the future, while others believe prophetic dreams are the subconscious preparing you for a likely outcome.

7. Recurring dreams: Recurring dreams refer to dreams that we repeatedly experience over a sleep session or multiple sleep sessions. Recurring dreams contain the same or similar imagery and sensations in prior occurrences and can also occur in the form of recurring nightmares. Multiple theories suggest that recurring dreams result from risk avoidance, internalized fears, or other unresolved issues.

VII

Dream Themes and thier Meanings

There are many different types of dream themes and various meanings and interpretations of each experience. Some common themes in dreams include:

1. Being chased: Dreaming of being chased can sometimes signal that you are running away from a problem rather than confronting and resolving it. These issues can include deadlines, financial decisions, or relationship woes.

2. Death: Dreaming of your death or the death of a loved one can signify change or transformation occurring in your life.

3. Falling: Falling off a surface or in the air is a common dream theme. Some researchers believe that falling in your dreams can signal anxiety, lack of control, loss of power, or feeling overwhelmed.

4. Flying: Not all dream themes are rooted in insecurity or anxiety. Dreaming about soaring through the air can

indicate a sense of power or control, allowing you to gain a higher perspective on things.

5. Loose teeth: Dreaming that your teeth are falling out can be a sign that you feel unsettled or unsure about an event or person in your life or facing a challenging decision.

6. Naked in public: Dreaming that you're in a public space without your clothes on can be a signal that you're feeling particularly vulnerable or unprotected and unsafe.

7. Sex: Dreaming about sex can signal that you desire a sense of security or simply be a form of wish fulfillment.

CONCLUSION

A dream is a product of our imagination, the sum of all the actions taken from our sleep, emotionally, psychologically, and mentally. It occurs at any time and in many ways. A dream has a lot of meaning and types. Dream defines scientifically, rationally, and verbally by those curious about it. Through its types, lucid and non-lucid dreams, daydreams, and nightmares we can categorize our dreams and easily understand them. Dreams also have four stages, it scientifically explains when and how dreams occur. By means of vivid images and brain waves, we got the idea that there is a pattern to follow to reach the explanations of dreams. All in all the ideas being explained and studied by many strengthen the fact that the brain penetrates and absorbs everything and dreams become its crop.

9 798887 831800

Printed by Libri Plureos GmbH in Hamburg,
Germany